GW01403316

International Terrorism

Nature, causes & resolutions

Hannah Young

What is this book about?

This book provides an in-depth overview and analysis of international terrorism. Using the most recent data and research available this book discusses the nature of terrorism in relation to the countries and regions most impacted, the most deadly terrorist organisations. It also analyses possible social, economic and political motivations for terrorism today. An evaluation of the impact of terrorism on individuals, families and communities is also included. The impact of terrorism on the international community is also discussed in relation to the building and breaking of political and economic relations. The book culminates with an in-depth analysis of the effectiveness of the responses by the UK Government and latterly the effectiveness of the United Nations, the European Union and the North Atlantic Treaty Organisation (NATO) in tackling international terrorism.

How can this book help you?

This book is ideal for anyone interested in learning more about international terrorism and helping make sense of current news stories and international relations. It is also ideal for students studying terrorism for SQA Modern Studies courses, International Baccalaureate Global Politics students and students considering applying to study Politics and International Relations at university.

THE NATURE OF INTERNATIONAL TERRORISM

A definition of terrorism

There is no universally accepted definition of terrorism. It remains the subject of continuing debate within the international community.

The UK Terrorism Act 2006 states that *"terrorism" means the use or threat of action where:*

- *the action involves serious violence against a person, serious damage to property, endangers a person's life, other than that of the person committing the action, creates a serious risk to the health or safety of the public or a section of the public, is designed seriously to interfere with or seriously to disrupt an electronic system*
- *the use or threat is designed to influence the government or an international governmental organisation or to intimidate the public or a section of the public*
- *the use or threat is made for the purpose of advancing a political, religious or ideological cause.*

The US PATRIOT Act of 2001 defined terrorist activities as:

• *threatening, conspiring or attempting to hijack airplanes, boats, buses or other vehicles.*

• *threatening, conspiring or attempting to commit acts of violence on any "protected" persons, such as government officials*

• *any crime committed with "the use of any weapon or dangerous device," when the intent of the crime is determined to be the endangerment of public safety or substantial property damage rather than for "mere personal monetary gain.*

In May 2011, President Barack Obama signed the PATRIOT Sunsets Extension Act, a four-year extension of three key powers: roving wiretaps, searches of business records, and conducting surveillance of "lone wolves"—individuals suspected of terrorist-related activities not linked to terrorist groups.

What is interesting to note is that not all US government departments share an agreed definition of terrorism. The FBI's definition of terrorism is *'the unlawful use of force or violence against persons or property to intimidate or coerce a government, the civilian population, or any segment thereof, in furtherance of political or social objectives.'* In contrast, the U.S. Army Manual definition of terrorism is the "*calculated use of unlawful violence or threat of unlawful violence to inculcate fear. It is intended to coerce or intimidate governments or societies ... [to attain] political, religious, or ideological goals."*

The United Nations does not have an internationally-agreed definition of terrorism. This international organisation is hindered by a definitional impasse about what constitutes terrorism and which groups should be designated as terrorists.

This is significant as it could be argued that without a consensus of what constitutes terrorism, the international community can not only unite against and tackle the issue, but there will be ways and means for some groups to evade the rule of law. When some terror organisations are funded by state actors, this issue is complicated further.

CASE STUDY: HEZBOLLAH

In 1985 the Shi'ite Islamic militant group, Hezbollah (Arabic for "*Party of God*") identified the US and the Soviet Union as Islam's principal enemies and called for the "*obliteration*" of Israel, which it said was occupying Muslim lands.

Hezbollah has been a prominent group in the political life of Lebanon since 1992. The group is anti-Israeli, pro-Syrian and since 2012 it has been fighting on behalf of Syria's President Bashar Assad in his country's civil war. According to the U.S. Treasury Iran is believed to fund

Hezbollah with up to $200 million per year. However, in the years after the Iranian nuclear deal was signed and the end to the thirty years of economic sanctions imposed on Iran, it has been reported that Iran has increased its financial support to Hezbollah to $800 million a year. Some of this financial support comes in the form of cash and weapons. Weapons supplied to Hezbollah by Iran include anti-aircraft and anti-ship missiles, as well thousands of anti-tank missiles, the Iranian made Zelzal-2 unguided long-range artillery rocket, Soviet made M-30 "Smerch" rockets and Scud missiles. The Washington Institute reported that Iranian cargo planes deliver these armaments to Hezbollah in regular flights to Damascus from Tehran. These weapons are offloaded in Syria and trucked to Hezbollah camps in Lebanon's Bekaa Valley.

Hezbollah have access to other sources of finance, notably from South America. In 2008 The Los Angeles Times reported that an international cocaine smuggling and money laundering ring had been uncovered. Other countries such as Mexico, Venezuela have also been accused of having financial links with Hezbollah.

The 2006 Lebanon War between Israel and Lebanon ended in stalemate, destruction and mass fatalities on both sides. One area of long-disputed territory is Shebaa Farms, a small strip of land at the intersection of the Lebanese-Syrian border and the Israeli-occupied Golan Heights. In 1981, the Golan Heights, including the Shebaa Farms, were annexed by Israel, a move not recognised by the international community. The United Nations designated the area a part of Syria, currently occupied by Israel. Hezbollah claims that it is Lebanese territory that Israel occupies illegally. The group does not recognise the State of Israel and has repeatedly targeted Israeli troops patrolling the area. Hezbollah has been a part of the Lebanese government since November 2005. On May 6, 2018, Lebanon held its first election since 2009. Hezbollah won 13 out of the 128 available seats in the Lebanese Parliament and remains the only Lebanese party with an active militia.

The question of the designation of Hezbollah as a terror group, military wing of a legitimate political party, freedom fighters or resistance movement is a contentious one. Hezbollah was designated as a foreign terrorist organisation (FTO) by the U.S. State Department since October 1997. In 2016, Saudi Arabia led Gulf countries and the Arab League to declare Hezbollah a terrorist group, accusing it of *'hostile acts'*. Israel and the EU consider Hezbollah to be a terrorist organisation. It is perhaps the case that Hezbollah is the 'puppet of Iran' and the group's actions are the result of state-sponsored terrorism. Some would argue that Hezbollah is assisting Iran in a proxy war with Israel. It could be argued that it may benefit countries like Israel and the US to designate the group as a terror organisation so that it can contain Iran's expanding influence in the Middle East which would impact negatively both Israel and the US.

In 2009, Jeremy Corbyn, leader of the UK Labour Party was challenged for describing terror groups Hezbollah and

Hamas (the Palestinian group which has called for the total annihilation of Israel) his "*friends*". In 2016 at a committee hearing on antisemitism in the Labour Party, Corbyn stated that he regretted his choice of words.

What is clear is that a universally accepted definition of terrorism does not exist. This poses problems when the international community tries to adopt a multilateral response to tackling this issue. If countries cannot arrive at a consensus about which groups are/are not terrorists and which acts are terroristic/hate crimes/political violence or legitimate political resistance, a cooperative and cohesive response will not occur.

The Global Terrorism Database (GTD), the most authoritative data source on terrorism today and the National Consortium for the Study of Terrorism and Responses to Terrorism (START) define terrorism as *'the threatened or actual use of illegal force and violence by a non-state actor to attain a political, economic, religious, or social goal though fear, coercion, or intimidation'.* This book will use this definition to determine the nature, causes and consequences of international terror groups and their activities.

Groups and their motivations

The Global Terrorism Index (GTI) reported that the four terrorist groups responsible for the most deaths in 2017 were the Islamic Sate of Iraq and the Levant (ISIL), The Taliban, Al-Shabaab and Boko Haram.

1.ISIL (also known as IS, Islamic State, ISIS and Daesh)

This group is motivated by a desire to establish a caliphate or autonomous Islamist state across the Middle East, southern Europe and North Africa. It is a Salafist jihadist militant group that adheres to a fundamentalist doctrine of Sunni Islam. Sunni Islam is the largest denomination of Islam and this group believes that the prophet Mohammed did not appoint a successor. Another Islamic denomination, Shia Muslims adhere to the belief that Mohammed appointed his cousin as his successor. This has resulted in religio-political tensions between the two Islamic factions. This schism has led to conflict and the rise of ultraconservative Islamic movements, notably, Wahhabism, which some claim has inspired the religio-political ideology of ISIL.

ISIL is driven by an ideology that incorporates both religious and political elements. The group has an intolerance of Christianity, Judaism and "diluted" Islamic groups. ISIL also reject democracy as it believes that such a political system cannot co-exist with Sharia Law.

The group's leader, Abu Bakr al-Baghdadi, also known as 'The Ghost' and 'The Invisible Sheik' is believed to be living in hiding in Hajin, a small city in eastern Syria, about 30 kilometres (18 miles) from the border with Iraq (although this former ISIL urban stronghold reportedly fell following intensive fighting by US-backed Kurdish-led soldiers on 14th December 2018. It is reported that approximately 5000 ISIL fighters remain in Hajin.) In 2016, the U.S. State Department offered a reward of up to $25 million for information or intelligence leading to the capture or death al-Baghdadi. US intelligence reports that al-Baghdadi sleeps in a suicide vest which he would detonate if faced with capture.

The group has enjoyed vast wealth. At the group's height there were reports of fortunes of $2 billion derived mainly from the revenue raised from sales of oil ($1 million per day by some estimations), ransoms from hostage taking and bank robbing (in June 2014 ISIL stole gold bullion reportedly worth $425 million from a bank in Mosul, Iraq).

The group uses bombings and explosions as its main tactics and favours social media platforms, such as YouTube and Twitter to encourage the radicalisation and recruitment of people all over the world.

2.Boko Haram

This group whose name translates as "western education is forbidden" was the world's deadliest terror group in 2014 (responsible then for 6,612 deaths) but has recently experienced a decline in impact. The group originated in northeast Nigeria and was initially non-violent, concerned predominately with the 'purification' of Nigeria and the promotion of Wahhabism, Salafism and Sharia Law. The group regards many other forms of Islam as idolatrous.

In March 2015 Boko Haram swore an allegiance to ISIL. Released via Twitter, the audio tweet stated: "*We swear our allegiance to the Caliph of the Muslims [Abu Bakr al-*

Baghdadi], and all hear and obey him in times of difficulty and prosperity, in hardship and in ease, and to endure being discriminated against..."

Boko Haram rejects westernisation in all its forms. It links westernisation with Christianity and points to the concentration of wealth in the Christian south of Nigeria. Nigeria accounts for 47% of West Africa's population, and has one of the largest youth populations in the world. Nigeria is Africa's biggest economy, although 60% of its population of 173 million (as of 2013) live on less than $1 (79p) a day. The World Bank reported in November 2018 that despite an average growth in GDP of 5.7% per year between 2006 and 2016, *"large pockets of Nigeria's population still live in poverty, without adequate access to basic services, and could benefit from more inclusive development policies. The lack of job opportunities is at the core of the high poverty levels, of regional inequality, and of social and political unrest in the country."*

The violent terroristic activities of the group have resulted in the displacement of around 2 million people from Nigeria. These refugees have fled to neighbouring Cameroon, Chad or Niger. These neighbouring states have also experienced the terror of Boko Haram as the group's influence has permeated across Nigeria's borders.

The group have carried out mass abductions including the kidnapping of 276 schoolgirls from Chibok in April 2014. In 2017 Boko Haram carried out 272 attacks which killed 1,254 people (a reduction of 82% since 2014). The group uses tactics of mass hostage takings and uses widely children and women as suicide bombers. Nearly four in five Boko Haram bombings in 2016 were suicide bombings with one in five committed by women.

3.The Taliban

The Taliban emerged in Afghanistan in 1994 as a reactionary group that combined both mujahideen (guerrilla fighters in Islamic countries, especially those who are fighting against non-Muslim forces) that had previously fought against the 1979 Soviet invasion, and groups of Pashtun tribesmen. The Taliban took control of Afghanistan in 1996. The group declared the country an Islamic emirate and promoted its leader to the role of head of state. Following the 2001 NATO invasion of Afghanistan, the Taliban was ousted, but it has since been steadily regaining control of its lost territory. As of mid-2017, it was estimated that the Taliban controlled over 11% of the country and contested another 29% of Afghanistan's 398 districts. In recent months, the Taliban has appeared receptive to peace talks, however fighting has continued.

The group's leader from 2015 was Mullah Mansour. Mansour was killed in a US drone strike in May 2016 and replaced by his deputy Mawlawi Hibatullah Akhundzada, a hard-line religious scholar. The Taliban claims that it is driven by a motivation to restore peace, security and Sharia Law in Pashtun areas of Pakistan and Afghanistan.

The Taliban has enjoyed strong and long-standing links with Pakistan. Many Afghans who initially joined the movement were educated in madrassas (religious schools) in Pakistan. It is a widely held belief that these religious schools which preached a fundamentalist form of Sunni Islam were funded by Saudi Arabia. Pakistan was also one of only three countries, along with Saudi Arabia and the United Arab Emirates (UAE), which recognised the Taliban when they were in power in Afghanistan from the mid-1990s until 2001. Pakistan was also the last country to break diplomatic ties with the Taliban.

The Taliban in Afghanistan were accused of providing a sanctuary to Osama Bin Laden and the al-Qaeda terror group which was blamed for the 9/11 attacks. Soon after 9/11 the Taliban were driven from power in Afghanistan by a US-led coalition.

In Taliban-controlled areas men were required to grow beards and women are to wear the all-covering burka. The Taliban banned television, music and cinema and disapproved of girls aged 10 and over from going to school.

One of the most internationally criticised of all Pakistani Taliban attacks took place in October 2012, when schoolgirl Malala Yousafzai was attacked on her way home in the town of Mingora. Yousafzai had been an outspoken advocate of women's education but as she became more well-known a Taliban spokesman said they were "*forced*" to act. In a meeting held in the summer of 2012, Taliban leaders unanimously agreed to kill her. Yousafzai survived the assassination attempt on a bus as she was travelling home after taking an exam. A year later she co-authored *I am Malala*, an international best seller and in 2014 was the co-recipient of the Nobel Peace Prize. The 2013, 2014 and 2015 issues of Time magazine featured her as one of the most influential people globally.

Unlike ISIL, the Taliban is active mainly in a single country. All of the 3,571 deaths and 699 terrorist attacks in 2017 occurred within Afghanistan. However, the Taliban's Pakistani affiliate group, Tehrik-i-Taliban Pakistan (TTP), was responsible for 233 deaths and 56 attacks in Pakistan in 2017, demonstrating a Taliban-related presence outside of Afghanistan. As a whole, terror attacks by the Taliban are becoming more deadly. The deadliest attack committed by the Taliban was from a suicide explosion in Gardez, Paktika, killing 74 people and injuring an additional 236 people. The majority of terrorism by the Taliban is committed in Afghanistan's southern provinces, but almost all districts in the country experienced attacks at some point in 2017.

In 2017, the Taliban switched focus from attacks on civilians, towards attacks on police and military personnel. Armed assaults and bombings were the most common type of attack used by the Taliban, accounting for 54% of all attacks.

4.Al-Shabaab

Active in East Africa since 2006, Al-Shabaab is a Salafist terror group which affiliated itself to Al Qa'ida in 2012. The group's name means *'Movement of Striving Youth'* or *'The Guys'*. The group has claimed responsibility for several deadly attacks concentrated around Somalia's capital city of Mogadishu and attacks in the neighbouring states of Kenya, Ethiopia and Uganda. The group is motivated by a desire to topple the Western-backed Somali Government. Its founder and spiritual leader, Ahmed Abdi Godane (who trained with the Taliban in Afghanistan) was confirmed killed by a US air strike in September 2014. The current leader or Emir, Ahmed Omar, has a bounty of $6,000,000 on his head from the US Rewards for Justice Program.

African Union peacekeeping forces known as AMISOM have been fighting Al-Shabaab since 2007 with the help of US and UN support. In 2017, the first wave of US troops and airstrikes were deployed in Somalia to fight Al-Shabaab. In 2017, Al-Shabaab overtook Boko Haram as the deadliest terror group in sub-Saharan Africa for the first time since 2010. The total number of deaths increased by 93 per cent from 2016 to 2017.

On 14 October 2017, Al-Shabaab committed the deadliest terror attack of the year through a suicide and truck-bombing targeting a hotel and highway intersection in Mogadishu, killing 588 and injuring 316 individuals. This bombing was the world's deadliest terror attack since 2014 and the fifth-deadliest terror attack since the year 2000.

The truck involved in this attack was packed with several hundred kilograms of military-grade and homemade explosives and is thought to have been targeting Somalia's foreign ministry.

Countries most impacted by terrorism

Terrorism is currently the biggest threat to national security that many countries currently face. The GTI reported in 2018 that while there was an overall decrease (by 27%) in the number of global terrorism related deaths, countries like Egypt and Somalia experienced significant increases in deaths. Deaths in these countries increased by 123% and 93% respectively. Al-Shabaab committed the deadliest attack of 2017, which killed 587 people while in Egypt, the Islamic State-Sinai Province (also known as ISIL-SP, is a militant Islamist group active in the Sinai Peninsula of Egypt) carried out the second deadliest attack, which killed 311 people.

The GTI also reported that the increase in the impact of terrorism was greatest in the Middle East and North Africa (MENA), followed by sub-Saharan Africa. Several countries in these regions are experiencing violent conflict, civil wars, unstable or corrupt governments, contain scarce natural resources and/or have poor human rights records. There may be a direct correlation between these pre-existing conditions in some countries and the rise and impact of terrorism. For example, Syrian President Beshar al-Assad, has been embroiled in a civil war in his country since March 2011. His forces and international allies are fighting against anti-government rebel groups and Salafi jihadist groups such as al-Nusra Front and ISIL. This conflict is part of a wider movement known as the Arab Spring which began in 2010 in Tunisia. This was a mass reaction to authoritarian governments, dictatorships, human rights violations and poverty among other issues. Such protest movements spread from Tunisia to Libya, Egypt, Yemen, Syria and Bahrain. In Syria, Assad is accused of gross human rights abuses and war crimes against his people. He is also a leader criticised for only representing a minority (17%) of the Syrian population, the Alawites, a secretive separate ethnoreligious group with different approaches to other followers of Islam. (For example, Alawites drink wine socially and in public and believe in reincarnation, unlike the majority of Muslims). As a result, Shia Islamic groups believe that the Alawites are *'ghulats'* or deviants. It would be fair to suggest that in countries, such as Syria, where people feel that they are under-represented politically, religiously, economically and socially, protest and terror groups can rise in vengeance. Of the countries impacted by the Arab Spring, all feature in the top 10 most impact countries by terrorism in 2016. Of the countries most impacted by terrorism in 2017 there is recent or current history of battles and/or conflicts. This is certainly the case for Iraq and Afghanistan which are ranked first and second respectively as the countries most impacted by terrorism in 2017.

Emerging trends in terrorism

Far-right terrorism is on the rise. The number of deaths from terrorism associated with far-right groups and individuals has increased from three in 2014, to 17 in 2017. The GTI reported that there were 66 deaths from terrorism caused by far-right groups and individuals from 113 attacks for the years from 2013 to 2017. Of those, 17 deaths and 47 attacks occurred in 2017 alone.

In Western Europe, there were 12 attacks in the UK, six in Sweden, and two each in Greece and France. In the US, there were 30 attacks in 2017 which resulted in 16 deaths. Most attacks were carried out by lone actors with far-right, white nationalist, or anti-Muslim beliefs.

The deadliest far-right terror attack was seen in Quebec City, Canada on 29 January 2017. Alexandre Bissonnette shot dead 6 and injured 19 worshippers at the Islamic Cultural Centre of Quebec City. Evidence points to Bissonnette's far-right, white-supremacist, ultra-nationalistic, anti-Muslim, anti-refugee and anti-feministic views. Although the act was condemned by Canadian Prime Minister, Justin Trudeau, as a terrorist attack, Bissonnette was not charged with terrorism, but instead 6 counts of first-degree murder. This is because in Canadian law, terrorism requires that terrorism is a violent act in collaboration with a terrorist group. Since Bissonnette was acting alone, terrorism was difficult to prove.

The Guardian reported in April 2018 that Bissonnette had told police officers that his actions were motivated by Trudeau's response to US President, Donald Trump's travel ban. This US Executive Order (13769) also known as *'Protecting the Nation from Foreign Terrorist Entry into the United States"* came into effect on 27 January 2017, just two days before Bissonnette's attack on the Quebec City mosque. This Order banned nationals from the Muslim-majority countries of Iran, Libya, Somalia, Sudan, Syria, and Yemen from entering the US. It also capped the number of refugees to be admitted into the United States in 2017 to 50,000. Under Obama this limit was set at 110,000. The justification for these restrictions was that the US government claimed that there was clear evidence that the aforementioned 7 countries were known to harbour terrorists. Bissonnette claimed that his attack was motivated by him being convinced that refugees were a threat to his family, especially in the light of Trudeau's response to the travel ban where he stated that refugees would be welcome in Canada.

On 27 October 2018, Robert Bowers who had expressed anti-Semitic views on social media, murdered 11 people in a Pittsburgh Synagogue. Shortly after his arrest he allegedly made anti-Semitic statements, telling one SWAT officer that he wanted all Jews to die and also that *"they (Jews) were committing genocide to his people."* CNN reported that Bowers' had commented on his Gab.com account that Jews were helping to transport members of the migrant caravans, calling them 'invaders'.

Far-right movements have grown in popularity and visibility in recent years. In Europe nationalist and far-right parties have made significant electoral gains. The current coalition government in Italy is made up of two populist parties – *Five Star Movement* and *The League*. Their joint manifesto includes plans for mass deportations for undocumented migrants. Italy's interior minister and League leader Matteo Salvini said the island must stop being "*the refugee camp of Europe*".

This surge in far-right political movements may give credence or legitimacy to terror groups that may share similar political beliefs. In early October 2018, 28-year-old far-right activist Luca Traini shot and wounded 5 men and one woman of African origin in the small town of Macerata in central Italy. When apprehended by police Traini was found wrapped in an Italian flag, in front of a monument to Italy's war dead, performing the Roman salute and screaming "*Viva l'Italia*".

A connection could be made between the recent rise in far-right political parties and far-right terrorist groups. In 2017, Germany saw the far-right Alternative for Germany (AfD) enter the federal Parliament, the Bundestag, for the first time. The leaders of the AfD have been accused of denying the atrocities of the Holocaust, Islamophobia and being anti-immigration. In early October 2018 German police arrested six men on suspicion of belonging to a far-right terrorist group that attacked foreigners in the city of Chemnitz. This city represents a stronghold for AfD and local police have experienced difficulties controlling the region's football hooliganism which in this case has strong links to neo-Nazism groups.

In Austria, the Freedom Party (FPÖ) only narrowly lost a presidential election and entered government as a junior partner within a coalition. In April 2018 the coalition government put forward proposals to seize refugees' cash and phones as well as speed up deportations. There have also been proposals to ban headscarves for girls aged under 10 in schools. In August 2018 a group of young Austrians belonging to the Indentitarian movement used a crane to dress Vienna's 65-foot statue of Empress Maria Theresa in a niqab. A poster next to the statue read, "*Islamization? No thanks!* '

Dubbed Europe's answer to the US's alt-right, the group has scaled the roof of the Greens' party headquarters in Graz, southern Austria, and stormed a theatre production performed by refugees in Vienna, handing out leaflets that read "*multiculturalism kills*." Martin Sellner, the Austrian Indentitarian's co-leader chartered a ship to "*defend Europe*," trying to stop migrants crossing the Mediterranean from Libya. While these acts have not directly resulted in death, some could be considered terroristic in nature given the group's threatened or actual use of illegal force and violence by a non-state actor to attain a political, economic, religious, or social goal though fear, coercion, or intimidation (the GTI definition). This is significant as it could be argued that as the far-right gain traction in the European political arena, confidence may grow amongst groups such as the Indentitarian movement as extremism becomes the new mainstream.

Cyberterrorism

Governments are becoming increasingly reliant on technology in order to create more efficient and streamlined infrastructures. It is the case that as terrorist groups develop, receive funding from state actors, or seek to disrupt a government system in order to create chaos and bring leaders and states to their knees, cyberterrorism can be an attractive offensive strategy. Even though cyberterrorism is not, physically violent in nature, it can cause significant damage to governments and citizens alike.

Targets of cyberterrorism can be industrial control systems, nuclear power stations, or as was experienced in May 2017, an attack on the National Health Service and FedEx. This global cyberattack was dubbed 'Wannacry'/ 'WanaCypt0r 2.0'/ 'WCry' and infected 300,000 computers mainly in Russia, Taiwan, Ukraine and India. This particular cyber terror attack was delivered by a virus-filled email which released malware onto computer systems in a technique known as phishing. The virus encrypts files on the infected computer and the cyberterrorists demand payment in Bitcoin to release files and for the user to regain access. This perhaps explains why Mikko Hypponen, chief research officer at the Helsinki-based cybersecurity company F-Secure, called the Wannacry attack "*the biggest ransomware outbreak in history.*"

In the UK, the NHS was targeted by Wannacry. This resulted in administrative chaos as patient files and other confidential documents were encrypted by the malware virus. People were advised to only seek medical assistance in emergencies due to the service's inability to process patients. Thousands of operations and other appointments were cancelled, and ransoms were demanded to restore access. The social cost to people's health is patent. The economic cost is also evident as figures revealed by the Department of Health and Social Care showed a total cost of £92m to the NHS.

In April 2017 a North Korean man, Park Jin Hyok, was identified as being behind the cyberattack. He was a member of the state-sponsored *'Lazarus Group'* which is also thought to be responsible for a similar cyberattack on Sony Pictures in 2014.

Another example of cyberterrorism was seen in relation to a group known as the Pakistani Cyber Army. This group, which does not claim to be a terror or hacking group, has been known to target Indian, Chinese, and Israeli companies and governmental organisations. The Pakistani Cyber Army are motivated by Pakistani nationalism and Islam. Members of this group have claimed responsibility for the hijacking of websites belonging to Acer, Indian telecommunications company, BSNL, India's Central Bureau of Investigation, Central Bank, and the State Government of Kerala.

THE CAUSES OF INTERNATIONAL TERRORISM

To what extent do economic factors cause international terrorism?

There are a number of economic causes of international terrorism. Some would argue that there is a direct link between poverty and terrorism. In 2014, former US Secretary of State John Kerry claimed that poverty *"in many cases is the root cause of terrorism."* However, a World Bank study on ISIL recruits shows that Kerry's claim is not entirely accurate. This study found that poverty is *not* a driver of radicalisation into violent extremism. New evidence suggests that socio-economic status is a poor indicator of how likely someone is to support terrorism because there are several countries that demonstrate high levels of poverty but do not generate significant problems related to terrorism, with Haiti being a case in point. The levels of poverty in Haiti are generally regarded as among the most severe in the western hemisphere, and yet it is ranked by the GTI as a country with some of the lowest levels of terrorism in the world. That said, Nigeria, the country with the world's highest number of people living in extreme poverty, (which is defined as living on less than $1.90 a day. 87 million people live in poverty in Nigeria compared to 70.6 million in the second ranked country, India) is ranked by the GTI as the 8th most impacted country by terrorism which may indicate a link between poverty and a cause of terror.

Terrorist groups are all too happy to step into a socio-economic void. They can offer salaries to their foot soldiers, so they can support their families. ISIL pay their fighters $500 per month and when this amount is compared to the average monthly salary in Iraq of $150, some individuals may join terror groups as a way out of the poverty that they face. This shows that economic factors may be a cause of terrorism because people must make a choice between surviving and not. ISIL offer social services—schools, health clinics—to do what local governments cannot or will not do. Therefore, people may choose to join or support terror groups so that they are able to gain an education and healthcare, and this indicates a politico-socio-economic motivation as the terror groups are acting as a de facto government providing a welfare state for socio-economically disadvantaged people.

A high proportion of young people in volatile countries, plus a dearth of economic opportunities, has long been considered a tinder box for extremism. In 2014, President Obama announced an expansion of entrepreneurship, education, and youth programs, because, he said, *"these investments are the best antidote to violence.*" It could certainly be argued that a lack of unemployment opportunities has a role to play in contributing to international terrorism because a disaffected youth that may feel hopeless, humiliated, lack self-esteem and faces few prospects for change and development may seek to join terror groups to give themselves a purpose in their lives. In 2017, Syria was ranked as having the highest levels of unemployment at 50% of its population. When we consider the fact that Syria is ranked by the GTI as the 4th country most impacted by terrorism, we might argue that there is a clear link between economic disadvantage and terrorism.

Research undertaken at Princeton University in 2002 provided evidence gathered from Hezbollah and Hamas suggesting that upper-middle class and more educated individuals are slightly over-represented in these pro-Palestinian organisations. This shows that it is over simplistic to suggest that poverty alone causes people to become terrorists or support terror organisations and that there may be other contributing factors.

Some Americans involved in terrorism have come from affluent backgrounds: Anwar Awlaki, the American cleric who took on a leadership role in Al Qaeda in the Arabian Peninsula, was the son of a major Yemeni political figure. Zachary Chesser who was born to a well-off family in the Virginia suburbs was sentenced to 25 years in prison for trying to join Al Shabaab and threatening the creators of South Park over their depiction of Mohammed. This shows that poverty could not have been a significant driving force behind their joining of terror groups because they were supposedly affluent. On the other hand, American Somalis—82% of whom live near or below the poverty line—are the source of the largest groups travelling to fight with jihadist groups abroad. The New York Times referred to the group of Minnesotans—most of whom were of Somali descent—that travelled to fight for Al Shabaab as *"the largest group of American citizens suspected of joining an extremist movement affiliated with Al Qaeda."* Since that report, the same communities have wrestled with a new wave of individuals travelling to fight in Syria. This shows that in these cases there is a potential link between poverty and terrorism, however other factors may also be significant for these individuals such as protection of their religious faith which they feel is under attack or possibly a dissatisfaction with the US and other western governments. Research findings indicate that social inequality among American Somali participants contributes to motivation to radicalise and join terror groups. The Trump administration has stepped up military efforts in Somalia, including dozens of drone strikes against al-Shabaab and this may be an additional political motivator for Somali-Americans to join Al Shabaab in retaliation for such foreign policy.

To what extent do social factors cause international terrorism?

Social Isolation

CASE STUDY: ANDERS BREIVIK

Some people that resort to terrorism, particularly lone wolf attackers, have backgrounds which suggest a lack of a sense of identity or belonging. An absence of social identity may result in an individual developing feelings of frustration with their society, government or country. If they feel that they are not represented or are under-represented by their government, they may feel that democratic avenues to express their views may be closed to them. People who are isolated in a society and want attention or recognition may resort to violence.

It is also possible that some people experiencing social isolation may be more susceptible to radicalisation. Often such vulnerable individuals are targeted on-line by those grooming potential terrorists.

Anders Breivik, responsible for the deaths of 77 people after planting a car bomb in Oslo and opening fire on a large number of young people at a political camp, was an individual who had become extremely isolated from society. He justified his 2011 terror attack as a response to what he declared as the *'Islamification of Norway'* and condemned the Norwegian and other European governments for embracing immigration and multiculturalism. He identified with a far-right political agenda and held strong Christian beliefs.

It has been reported by Journal EXIT-Deutschland that Breivik was a dedicated online gaming enthusiast. Playing online fantasy games such as *World of Warcraft* dominated his daily life during the years leading up to the attacks. Lengthy periods of time playing games resulted in him being isolated from friends and relatives. The subject of these games may have also contributed to his violence terroristic act. Breivik admitted that multiplayer role-playing fantasy games was practically his entire occupation for a whole year. He was also an active participant in online forums focused on far right or anti-Muslim views.

The *Perspectives on Terrorism* journal reported in 2011 that such was his revulsion towards his family that he wore an antiseptic mask around his house. Psychologists have commented that Breivik shows a very high level of self-obsession and narcissism. *The Telegraph* reported in 2011 that he had plastic surgery to look more Aryan. A common theme in his writings is how attractive he believed himself to be.

Islamophobia

The perceived increase in attacks by Islamic extremists has resulted in a surge of violent Islamophobic incidents. Islamophobia is defined as the *'dread or hatred of Islam and therefore, (the) fear and dislike of all Muslims'*. Some individuals may feel that their culture, faith, beliefs or identity is under threat or is actively being attacked and this may lead to such individuals carrying out attacks in defence of what they hold to be true.

Islamophobic attacks increased by 500% in Greater Manchester after the ISIL-inspired terror attack on an Ariana Grande concert in the city in 2017 in which 23 people were killed (including bomber Salman Ramadan Abedi, a 22-year-old British-born citizen of Libyan descent) with around 120 injured. Think tank, *Demos*, reported that almost 7,000 Islamophobic tweets were sent worldwide in the English language every day in July 2016, with the vast majority in Europe coming from the UK. Demos stated that the highest number of Islamophobic tweets sent in a single day - 21,190 - came on July 15, the day after Mohamed Salmene Lahouaiej-Bouhlel drove a lorry into crowds celebrating Bastille Day in Nice, killing 85 people.

Chief Superintendent Dave Stringer, Scotland Yard's head of community engagement commented in February 2018 that the number of Islamophobic hate crimes in London had soared by almost 40% in the past year. There were 1,678 anti-Muslim hate crimes reported in the capital in the year up to January 2018 – up from 1,205 reported in 2017.

CASE STUDY: THE FINSBURY PARK MOSQUE ATTACK

The Finsbury Park Mosque attack of June 2017 is an example of Islamophobic terrorism, where several worshippers were struck by a hired van driven by Darren Osborne, a 47-year-old man from Cardiff. A witness reported that Osborne shouted *'I want to kill all Muslims'* before he was intercepted by onlookers and the police. This led to Finsbury Park Mosque chairman Mohammed Kozbar requesting that all Islamophobic attacks be classed as terrorism. According to the US extremist monitoring group, *Site*, white supremacists celebrated the attack. It also claimed that pro-Islamic State channels were using reports of the incident to incite Muslims. This is significant as it shows that when people feel that their faith and sites of religious worship are targeted in this violent manner, they may well retaliate. When some people believe that their faith, beliefs, culture and identity are under attack the message of terror groups such as ISIL become more relevant to them. ISIL requires its followers to defend Islam against attack. Individuals susceptible to radicalisation are more likely to resort to terrorism if they feel that acts of terroristic violence are the only way to seek vengeance.

Targeted Radicalisation

Terrorist groups have specifically targeted individuals and groups that they believe will be most amenable to radicalisation. Groups such as ISIL use the internet to engage vulnerable people in their rhetoric and encourage them either to travel to Syria or carry out atrocities in their own nations.

Social media is used to recruit, radicalise and raise funds. The attraction of social media tools is that they are cheap and accessible; identities can be hidden using encryption tools. Posts about accomplishments of the terror group (true or otherwise), can be shared quickly and far and wide. Publication of such information circumvents the need to filter through traditional news outlets.

The Taliban has been active on Twitter since May 2011 and has many thousands of followers. The group tweets frequently, on some days nearly hourly. Social-media monitor *Recorded Future* found that ISIL had succeeded in creating hype with a total of 700,000 Twitter accounts discussing the terrorist group.

Videos and images are shared by ISIL foot soldiers, are shared globally and immediately both by ordinary users and mainstream news organisations. The UK Government reported in 2015 that ISIL uses social media to incite radicalisation and support for the group. Images suggesting an exciting life are shared with the post description, *'Baqiyah wa-Tatamaddad'* (remaining and expanding) which presents the group as one that consistently achieves success.

ISIL propaganda depicts its caliphate as an ideal, utopian state where Muslims will find status and belonging. This could serve as a particularly attractive message to individuals feeling isolated and facing anti-Muslim messages in the media and on the streets. ISIL taps into the notion that it is the duty of Muslim men and women in the West to travel there and regularly states that all foreigners are welcome in its ranks, so long as they are Sunni Muslims.

People considering travel to Syria or Iraq sometimes use Ask.fm to ask British jihadis and female ISIL supporters about travel, living standards, recruitment, fighting and broader ideology. The answers given by ISIL supporters are encouraging, saying all their difficulties will be solved if they travel to the region. Instagram is used by fighters and ISIL supporters to share the photosets frequently produced by various ISIL media organisations. ISIL supporters also use Instagram to share pictures of their life in Syria, often showing landscapes and images suggesting they are living a full and happy life. Hashtags are used to create a buzz and following.

Tumblr, the blogging site, is exploited by fighters to promote longer, theological arguments for travel. Tumblr is popular with female ISIL supporters, who have written blogs addressing the concerns girls have about travelling to the region, such as leaving their families behind and living standards in Syria. ISIL supporters frequently encourage others to message them on closed or encrypted peer-to-peer networks, such as WhatsApp, Kik, SureSpot and Viber, when asked for sensitive information, such as on how to travel to the region, what to pack and who to contact when they arrive.

In Western countries such as the France and the UK there are examples of the isolation of Muslim communities which makes disenfranchised youth ripe for radicalisation. The demonisation of all Muslims as a dangerous 'other' group polarises communities and creates societal divisions creating a 'them' and 'us' narrative. This is notable as this is a desirable narrative for groups such as ISIL, Al Shabaab and Boko Haram. It provides justification to become radicalised and prepared to die to defend their faith. When their own followers die, ISIS uses martyrdom as powerful tool to convince the target audience that the cause is worth suffering and dying for. Martyrs become heroes who are publicly celebrated and recognised on the Internet.

To what extent do political factors cause international terrorism?

Terrorism is often considered *'the continuation of politics by other means'*. It would be fair to state that political factors are a significant driving force behind the actions of the most prolific terror groups around the world in recent years. Political factors cover a plethora of ideas, such as feelings of political under-representation or total lack of representation, corrupt governments, abuses of human rights, civil wars, other countries' foreign policies towards the country inhabited or protected by a terror group, marginalisation of groups, the preservation of terra sancta (sacred land) dissatisfaction with globalisation, unemployment, poverty, lack of education or opportunity and historic political grievances, such as a imperialism and colonialism.

CASE STUDY: HISTORIC AND CURRENT POLITICAL GRIEVANCES

In 1916 the British, French and Russian governments colluded to divide up the Ottoman Empire in the event of an Allied victory in the First World War. Once the Ottoman Empire was drawn into the war the Entente powers (Britain, France and Russia) assumed that the Ottoman Empire would be defeated so they took it upon themselves to divide up the lands taking great swathes of Middle East to add to their Empires. Taking a ruler and without considering the various tribes, languages, faiths and socio-political structures that pre-existed this action, a line was drawn dividing the Middle East into zones of western influence and control. This action was known as the Asia Minor Agreement, or more commonly known as the Sykes-Picot Agreement. British diplomat Sir Mark Sykes and French representative Francois Georges-Picot worked together to allocate territory and zones of influence to Britain, France, Russia and Italy. Palestine was allocated a 'special' international administration.

Under the Sykes-Picot Agreement control of Syria, Lebanon and Turkish Cilicia was handed over to the French. Northern Syria and Mesopotamia were also considered to be an area of French influence. Jordan and areas around the Persian Gulf and Baghdad were allocated to the British. Arabia and the Jordan Valley were also considered to be British spheres of influence. The deal failed to adequately consider the ethnic and religious divisions within the various countries they created, thus furthering the potential for conflict and desire for vengeance.

It is undeniable that such imperialistic ambitions and disregard for the sovereignty of the Ottoman Empire led to centuries of resentment which resonate today. When the Bolshevik-led government uncovered a copy of the Sykes-Picot Agreement in 1917 in the archives of the then overturned Romanov dynasty, it was published by Trotsky in the Party's newspaper, Pravda, and declared by Lenin to be *"the agreement of the colonial thieves"*.

In 2014, ISIL militants declared their intention to eradicate all the region's frontiers and lay Sykes-Picot to rest forever. In July 2014, Abu Bakr Al-Baghdadi stated, *"This blessed advance will not stop until we hit the last nail in the coffin of the Sykes–Picot conspiracy"*. ISIL removed border posts between Iraq and Syria, as part of the group's plan to restore the Islamic Caliphate on the ruins of the Sykes-Picot border.

It is the case that this treaty along with the Balfour Declaration of 1917 (a public statement written by UK Foreign Secretary Arthur Balfour during World War I (November 1917) announcing support for the establishment of a *"national home for the Jewish people"* in Palestine, then an Ottoman region with a small minority Jewish population) were interpreted by many as a manifestation of western greed, arrogance and misplaced authority. One could argue that the dilution of Palestine by the Balfour Declaration and the dispersal of Palestinians to make way for a Jewish population has resulted in the Arab-Israeli conflict which continues unabated today. It has also given rise to groups such as Hamas which conducts political and terroristic activities in the Gaza Strip against Israel. The Gaza Strip is situated on the eastern coast of the Mediterranean Sea, that borders Egypt on the southwest and Israel on the east and north. Hamas came to power following the 2007 elections there and since that time has faced an Israeli and U.S.-led international economic and political boycott. The Gaza strip is weakened as a result.

In May 2018 US President Donald Trump moved the US Embassy building from Tel Aviv to Jerusalem. This was perceived by Palestinians and much of the international community as provocative since both Palestinians and Israelis claim Jerusalem as their capital. Palestinian President Mahmoud Abbas called it a "*slap in the face*" and said the United States can no longer be regarded as an honest broker in any peace talks with Israel.

The State of Palestine is recognised by 137 out of 193 (71%) UN members (UN members that do not recognise Palestine include Israel, the United States, Canada, Japan, South Korea, Mexico, Australia and New Zealand. Most of the European Union do not recognise Palestine as a separate independent state. That said, a number of these UN members and EU member states do support a 'two-state solution'. Since November 2012 the State of Palestine has had non-member observer state status in the United Nations. (The only other non-member observer in the UN is the Holy See, the universal government of the Catholic

Church, which operates from the Vatican City State. The Holy See does not represent the Vatican City alone. It is the Holy See, not the Vatican City that maintains diplomatic relations with states.) 31 countries do not recognise Israel, notably, Lebanon, Iran, Saudi Arabi, Cuba and Pakistan.

Conflict between Israelis and Palestinians has resulted in mass loss of life and fractured diplomatic relations. Given that Israel is recognised as a state by the majority of the international community, any violent action it takes against Palestinian people, Hamas or Hezbollah cannot be declared terroristic in nature. The Israeli government defend their aggressive military actions as legitimate political violence against a group of people that have encroached on their land and are violent towards a recognised nation state. As Palestine is recognised by fewer UN member states than Israel, often its actions are denounced as terroristic. This is one of the difficulties with the definitional impasse surrounding the word 'terrorism' within the international community.

The defence of *terra sancta* meaning 'sanctified land', is often considered to be a cause of terrorism. Territory that is believed to belong to a group of people, is their homeland or the site of an important event must be protected and defended as it is not divisible and cannot be shared. As a result, some groups feel driven to fight for what they feel is their right. Negotiation is not possible as symbolically this territory is too important and sacred. This is certainly true when one considers the case of Jerusalem in the context of the Arab-Israeli conflict. Palestine and Israel view each other as the encroacher, the invader, the contaminator of their precious and important land. When religious faith and political grievances are mixed together, the result is a heady cocktail which can erupt at any moment. Tensions have been high for over 70 years and although a 'two-state solution' has been discussed, it would require considerable compromise on both sides.

Current western foreign policy is also a driver of politically motivated terrorism. The 2003 invasion of Iraq and the subsequent rise of ISIL is a case in point. The US-led Operation Iraqi Freedom entered Iraq justified by (the now unfounded) the premise that the then-leader Saddam Hussein was concealing Weapons of Mass Destruction (WMD). Hussein was killed, and his supporters were imprisoned in a detention centre called Camp Bucca in southern Iraq. A number of these inmates had previously been incarcerated in the notorious Abu Ghraib prison where abuse of prisoners at the hands of US officers had been uncovered. Incidents of torture techniques such as prolonged isolation, nudity, the use of loud music and noise, waterboarding and sleep deprivation were reported.

ISIL's current leader al-Baghdadi was incarcerated in Camp Bucca and it is likely that this detention centre became a hotbed of prisoner radicalisation. Many of these inmates were made up of the remnants of Saddam Hussein's military and alienated Sunni Muslims in Iraq. It is certainly the case that prisons are known to be hubs of radicalisation and this is no exception. What fuelled this radicalisation to a heightened level, however, was the vengeance sought at western intervention in Iraq, both current and historic. In addition, the humiliating treatment that many inmates claim to have suffered at the hands of US prison guards spurred many on to seek revenge. Expert in the study of terrorism, Professor Martha Crenshaw wrote in 1981 that *"if there is a single common emotion that drives the individual to become a terrorist, it is vengeance on behalf of comrades"*. It would fair to evaluate that ISIL have led a rallying cry or clarion call to potential followers to defend their shared faith which they believe to be under attack and must be defended.

CASE STUDY: NATIONALISM

Nationalism can manifest itself as an extreme form of patriotism marked by a feeling of superiority over other countries. One example of a terrorist group motivated by extreme nationalism is the Irish Republican Army (IRA). Irish republicanism is the belief that all of Ireland should be a republic independent of British rule.

The goal of the unionist and overwhelmingly Protestant majority is to remain part of the United Kingdom. The goal of the nationalist and republican, almost exclusively Catholic, minority was to become part of the Republic of Ireland.

What is now the Republic of Ireland released itself from British rule following the Anglo-Irish Treaty of December 1921 which gave Ireland independence with regards domestic and foreign affairs. An opt-out clause allowed

Northern Ireland to remain within the United Kingdom. The opt out was exercised and Northern Ireland became a province of the United Kingdom and therefore subject to the sovereignty of the Westminster Parliament.

The Province of Northern Ireland was formed in 1921 however this has led to a tumultuous conflict between groups that continue to seek independence from British authority and those that seek union with the United Kingdom. Starting in the late 1960s and continuing for 30 years, a period known as *The Troubles* became synonymous with the territorial battle over political sovereignty of Northern Ireland.

Operation Demetrius was a British Army operation that took place in Northern Ireland on 9–10 August 1971, during a period of time known as *The Troubles*. It involved the arrest and internment (imprisonment without trial) of 342 people suspected of being involved with the Irish Republican Army (IRA), which was striving for a united Ireland against the British state. The IRA was motivated by a desire for nothing less than immediate British withdrawal from Northern Ireland.

This conflict which still exists today is fuelled by nationalistic sentiment, feelings of political injustice and oppression, underrepresentation and religious divisions.

THE IMPACT OF INTERNATIONAL TERRORISM

In what ways are individuals, families and communities impacted by international terrorism?

CASE STUDY: NIGERIA

International terrorism has a significant negative impact on individuals, families and communities. One area in which this can be seen is in relation to the fear and loss that people living in areas such as Nigeria can face on a daily basis. As a result of the actions of terror group, Boko Haram, many people have experienced arson attacks on their homes, schools and hospitals. This has had a negative impact on individuals, families and communities as many people have lost their lives, become homeless, are unable to attend school or receive medical attention all which can result in feelings of hopelessness, destitution and ultimately, death. Mass migration, both internal and external, can also result in generational refugeeism which can be a difficult cycle to break

Hundreds of thousands of children across the Lake Chad Basin have been denied their right to education because of Boko Haram violence and destruction. The distress of conflict and lack of schooling is likely to seriously affect their outlook and opportunities. Access to education has been particularly affected in north-east Nigeria, where the worst of the attacks have taken place. It could be argued that without education and resultant future prospects, children are at risk of being seen as an ideal recruitment pool for extremist organisations or criminal gangs and this would clearly have a negative impact on individuals and families.

Over a million people in the region have been displaced from their homes, often having been forced to move from community to community, making it difficult to keep their children in school. Others, particularly the families of girls, avoid school due to the high risk of abduction by the group. In April 2014, 276 female students were kidnapped from a school in town of Chibok in Borno State, Nigeria. 57 of the schoolgirls managed to escape in the subsequent months. A further 21 girls were freed in October 2016, one girl was rescued in November and another one in January 2017. 82 more girls were freed in May 2017 and one in January 2018. 113 remain unaccounted for. Those that returned home told of their experiences of rape, torture and enslavement. Now back in education, these girls face restrictions on their freedoms. They are unable to leave their university campus without an escort and have rarely seen their families since their return. This will have had a detrimental impact on their families who must seek special permission to spend time with their daughters and help them through a very traumatic experience in their lives. The Nigerian Government have placed strict controls on these women in order, it claims, to protect them. The negative psychological impact of the abduction on these women may be long term and they may experience poor mental and physical health as a result. Children born to these women during their period in captivity have been removed and this will also have been an incredibly difficult experience to deal with as young women.

In February 2018, in the nearby town of Dapchi another 110 schoolgirls were abducted by Boko Haram. This shows that the threat of abduction remains and as a result individuals, families and communities will be living in constant feat of attack which means that they will be living precarious lives with a fragile sense of safety and security.

Violent deaths are also a significant effect on individuals, families and communities. More than 20,000 people have been killed and more than two million have fled their homes since Boko Haram launched an armed campaign in 2009 to create an Islamic state in northeast Nigeria. Furthermore, health services are badly hampered leading to a great deal of avoidable suffering. A lack of healthcare provision will result in lower life expectancy, higher infant mortality rates and poor childhood health as a result of an absence of a comprehensive vaccination programme.

Without adequate education provision, Nigeria will suffer from and an inability to create prosperity through investment and growth. This will directly impact its GDP and ability to attract foreign investment which will have repercussions as it will have a negative effect on employment opportunities and income for individuals.

CASE STUDY: ISLAMOPHOBIA

Islamophobia can affect negatively individuals, families and communities as it can make Muslims feel as though their faith is under attack. Over 200,000 Islamophobia tweets were sent throughout the EU in July 2016 – an average of 289 per hour, according to think tank, *Demos*.

The impact of this on individuals, families and communities is that Muslims can feel that they are under siege and unwelcome. Some people that feel that their identity is under attack may even become radicalised in an attempt to fight the hostility and racial and religious hatred they are faced with. In a perverse twist therefore, Islamophobia may not only be an effect of terrorism, but it may also be the cause of some people being recruited to terrorist organisations and carrying out terror attacks in response to the discrimination they face.

It has been claimed that the UK Government's Prevent strategy has also had a negative impact on the Muslim community. Schedule 7 of the Terrorism Act 2000 allows stop and search to be carried out to question any person, for up to 9 hours in order to determine if they are involved in terrorism. There is no need for 'reasonable suspicion' before a person is stopped. Suspects are interviewed by UK authorities and have been asked questions directly related to their faith and understanding of the term 'jihad'. Since 2001 there have been over half a million stop and searches in the street using powers of the Terrorism Act. In addition, areas such as Birmingham have experienced a rise in the number of CCTV in areas densely populated by Muslims. The impact of the use of these powers has been largely negative and has resulted in the erosion of the trust that some Muslims have had in the police and Government. Some Muslims report that they feel that they are perceived as a 'suspect community' that faces hostility, fear and suspicion from non-Muslims. This has had a negative impact and resulted in the polarisation of different groups in society which has led to the decline in law and order and social cohesion.

In what ways are countries and the international community impacted by international terrorism?

SOCIAL IMPACT

Case Study: Australia.

One social effect of terrorism on countries and their governments is a break down in law and order. Australia has experienced significant social problems following a rise in the number of anti-Islamic protests in cities such as Melbourne & Sydney. These protests have been met with 'anti-racism' marches. The groups have clashed violently in the streets. Threats made against Australia by ISIL have also fuelled such protests. This is significant because it shows that the Australian government has had to increase the police presence on the streets of major cities. This will be at considerable cost to the tax payer and may divert spending away from other vital services such as hospitals and schools. Such protests could place pressure on overstretched police services and even make police a target for violence as representatives of the state.

The Australian government have tried to focus on easing tensions with the Islamic community however it has faced difficulties particularly from a far-right group that has been campaigning to have Islam banned in Australia. Anti-Islam Reclaim Australia Rallies have been held across Australia since 2015. Reclaim Australia is a far-right Australian nationalist protest group which is associated with neo-Nazi hate groups. The group have held street rallies in cities across Australia to protest against Islam. This is an important social effect that Australia must deal with in order to create greater social cohesion. A cohesive society is one where people are protected against life risks, trust their neighbours and the institutions of the state and can work towards a better future for themselves and their families. Fostering social cohesion is an essential role of a government as it is the glue that holds society together and reduces the risk of societal unrest. It is also important to consider that research suggests that protest movements can have a significant impact on elections. The Australian government has a difficult balance to maintain: on the one hand ensure law and order and on the other, allow freedoms of speech and assembly. Both will be important as the Prime Minister seeks re-election while other political parties could exploit a poor record of law and order to their political advantage in an election campaign.

A survey published in 2014 found that a quarter of Australians held anti-Muslim views; this incidence was five times higher than that for any other religion. This survey also found that 27% of Muslim Australians have experienced discrimination, which was also the highest of any of the religions covered in the study. Islamophobia poses a significant problem for countries and the international community as a whole as it is often perpetuated by fear and a sense that Muslims are taking over jobs, homes and lives, thus leading to a polarising society and the so-called clash of civilizations. This will only have a negative impact on communities as it is a divisive issue that can result in a break down in law and order which governments would need to tackle.

Case study: Nigeria and its neighbours

Acts of terror can cause poverty and homelessness as people's homes can be bombed by groups such as Boko Haram. The Boko Haram insurgency has displaced nearly 2.4 million people in the Lake Chad Basin. Although the Nigerian military has regained control in parts of the country's north-east, civilians in Nigeria, Cameroon, Chad and Niger continue to be affected by grave violations of human rights, widespread sexual and gender-based violence, forced recruitment and suicide bombings. Despite the efforts of governments and humanitarian aid organisations in 2017, some 4.5 million people remain food insecure and will depend on assistance. This is significant because the government must respond to the needs of its people especially in relation to conflict-induced food insecurity and severe malnutrition, which have risen to critical levels in all four countries. The impact of this is that these governments will face a humanitarian crisis, health pandemics, famine and a large refugee population living in poverty which will have a detrimental effect on the birth and death rates and ultimately the future potential of the countries themselves.

A further issue is the potential deterioration of relationships between these countries. Nigeria's neighbours have criticised her tackling of the terror threat of Boko Haram. They believe that had Nigeria taken a swift approach Boko Haram would not have been able to permeate across the borders into other countries. This has resulted in dissatisfaction towards the Nigerian Government. A border crossing between Cameroon and Chad was closed in May 2014 following a deadly attack on a border police station that Cameroonian officials blamed on Boko Haram. Nigeria has often accused Cameroon of not doing enough to fight Boko Haram as the terrorist group frequently crosses into Cameroonian territory. Cameroon has been attacked several times by Boko Haram. Border closures after attacks in Nigeria in 2012 to prevent further infiltration by Boko Haram had a negative impact on the Cameroonian economy as cross-border trade has declined. The Chadian economy has also been impacted negatively by border closures in an attempt to prevent the spread of Boko Haram. That said, Cameroon, Chad and Nigeria have cooperated in the quest to find and return the Chibok schoolgirls captured by Boko Haram in 2014 which shows that terrorism can actually result in stronger international relations through cooperation by fighting a common enemy.

ECONOMIC IMPACT

Foreign Direct Investment

CASE STUDY: NIGERIA

Terrorism can have a detrimental impact on a country's economy. Threats and acts of terrorism can lead to high levels of uncertainty for potential investors and this can result in a decline in Foreign Direct Investment (FDI). If terrorism reduces the flow of FDI, especially in developing nations, the growth and development of such countries will be stymied. Nigeria is a case in point. According to the main U.N. body dealing with trade, investment and development issues, UNCTAD, FDI flows to Nigeria dropped by 21% to reach 3.5 billion USD in 2017, Estimated at USD 97.6 billion, the total stock of FDI represents 24.4% of the country's GDP. Therefore, FDI is incredibly important to the buoyancy of the Nigerian economy and any decline in investment, whether it be capital, expertise or technological, will hamper Nigeria's growth.

According to bank, Santander, there are a number of obstacles to FDI in Nigeria, such as poorly developed transport and energy infrastructure, which result in high operating costs; inefficient government institutions and corruption; an inefficient judicial system and unreliable dispute settlement mechanisms; a high tax burden; a restrictive trade policy; and an increasing lack of security, especially in connection with the extremist group Boko Haram operating in the north-east of the country.

Therefore, while terrorism may have a negative economic impact on Nigeria, it must also be said that there are numerous pre-existing conditions in the country that also contribute to reductions in FDI.

CASE STUDY: IRAQ

Despite the current security challenges that Iraq faces in relation to ISIL, the country remains an attractive investment prospect for some foreign governments and organisations. Iraq has the fifth largest proven oil reserves in the world and requires tremendous reconstruction and infrastructure development post-2003 invasion. U.S. companies in particular have invested in security, energy, environment, construction, healthcare, agriculture, and infrastructure sectors. Despite the current crises in Iraq, hydrocarbons continue to draw in foreign companies, and the majority of FDI goes to the oil industry. That said, since 2013 the FDI inflow has been negative, reaching -5 billion USD in 2017. Therefore, the total FDI stock currently stands at USD 10.1 billion, around 5.3% of GDP (UNCTAD 2018 World Investment Report). The United States and the EU are the leading investors in Iraq: the stock of FDI from the U.S. was USD 1.6 billion in 2015, a 37.4% decrease the previous year. This shows that although FDI may have declined in Iraq in recent years, FDI still flows into this country. It may also be the case that Iraq may have suffered from a reduction in foreign investment not just as a result of terrorism, but also political instability and concerns about social stability. Corruption, obsolete infrastructure, a lack of skilled labour and outdated commercial laws may have also hindered investment.

Damage to the tourism industry

CASE STUDY: TUNISIA

Terrorism can have a negative impact on the tourism industry. The 2015 Sousse Attacks which saw 38 tourists (30 of whom were British) gunned down on a Tunisian beach by ISIL-inspired gunman, Seifeddine Rezgui, is a case in point. The attacks took a heavy toll on the country's tourism sector, which accounts for around 8% of GDP and provides employment for more than 200,000 people (13.8% of total employment in Tunisia. According to CNN, visitor numbers fell by 25% to 5.4 million in 2015, and revenue from tourists dropped by 35% to $1.1 billion. The economic impact of terrorism on Tunisia is clear. This attack, at least in the short-term resulted in mass unemployment and business closures, ultimately causing poverty, homelessness and migration. In 2018 tour European operators resumed flights and holiday packages to Tunisia and as a result the Tunisian Tourism Minister, Salma Loumi, predicted an 8 million forecast of tourist numbers which is higher than the pre-attack level of 7.1 million in 2014. Loumi claims that tourism revenues would increase by 25% compared to those in 2017. This shows that some countries can suffer the negative economic impact from individual terror attacks but have the ability to recover if they are not considered to have long-term terror threats and frequent attacks.

CASE STUDY: EGYPT

Egypt has experienced long–term difficulties associated with terrorism. Listed by the GTI as the 11th most impacted country by terrorism in the world, Egyptian security forces have dealt with three terrorist attacks on tourist locations in recent years. On 14 July 2017, three foreign tourists were killed, and several others injured following a knife attack at beach resorts in Hurghada. Attacks also took place in Luxor in June 2015 and in Hurghada in January 2016, without loss of life. The UK Government have offered advice on travelling to Egypt and state that *"there is a threat of kidnapping by groups operating in North Africa, particularly from Libya and Mauritania. This includes Al Qaeda in the Islamic Maghreb (AQ-IM) and Daesh-affiliated groups, who may travel across the region's porous border."* This shows that the economies of countries such as Egypt may be disproportionately affected by terrorism. This is because the perception from foreign governments and tourists could be largely negative as they may consider Egypt too dangerous a country in which to holiday. The long-term problems within Egypt of political and social instability only serve to bolster such a negative impression of this country and this too, will contribute to an economic downturn.

CASE STUDY: THE UK

In 2017 there were four terror attacks in the UK, three of which happened in the capital, killing more than 30 people. The Westminster attack where Khalid Masood drove a car into pedestrians on Westminster Bridge, killing four and injuring almost fifty is perhaps the most infamous. Masood then ran into the grounds of the Palace of Westminster and fatally stabbed a police officer.

The London Bridge attack is another example. Three men drove a van into pedestrians on London bridge before stabbing people in and around pubs in nearby Borough Market. Eight people were killed and at least 48 wounded. All three terrorists were wearing fake suicide bomb vests. The Finsbury Park attack enacted by Darren Osborne, a 47-year-old British man, who drove a van into Muslim worshippers near Finsbury Park Mosque, London is yet another example. A man who had earlier collapsed and was receiving first aid died at the scene.

Despite these terror attacks 2017 was a record year to date for visitors to the UK in general and London in particular, with growth set to continue throughout 2018-19. Visit Britain reported that there were 30.2 million visits to the UK from overseas in the first nine months of 2017, up 7% on the same period in 2016. This shows that acts of terror may have an impact on tourism in the short term in countries with higher levels of political and social stability however in the long term, these countries are considered by the public to be less dangerous and more desirable to visit because they are less volatile. Therefore, the economic impact may not be as significant or negative in such countries.

POLITICAL IMPACT

Divisions about the definition of terrorism.

The threat of terrorist activity is a major national security risk for many countries. It could be argued that the most significant effect of terrorism on the international community is the division over an agreed definition of terrorism. This definitional impasse is a result of each country having its own definition of terrorism, which causes divisions over what constitutes as illegitimate and legitimate political violence. For example, Hezbollah, an organisation which uses political violence against the Israeli government, has raised questions as to what constitutes as terrorism and which groups are terrorists. This has had a significant effect on the international community as it has hindered global cooperation and has prevented the implementation of a unified counter terrorism response.

The United Nations Security Council

The UN Security Council has a role to promote peace and security across the world. The UNSC has five permanent members, the victors of World War Two, and a number of non-permanent members, which are selected on a rotational basis. The UNSC has been criticised for only protecting the interests of a power body that is no longer representative of global powers. In addition, the USA has faced criticism of blocking any anti-Israeli resolutions. This has proved divisive for some member states and observer member states, such as Palestine, as Israeli interpretations of the threat of groups such as Hamas and Hezbollah are prioritised by the USA. Draft resolutions put forward in the Security Council that may have a negative impact on Israel are vetoed by the USA. Since 1972, the US Government has vetoed anti-Israeli action 39 times.

Military Coalitions

1. Combined Joint Task Force – Operation Inherent Resolve

Established in October 2014, the US Department of Defense formally established the *Combined Joint Task Force - Operation Inherent Resolve* (CJTF-OIR) in order to coordinate ongoing military actions against the rising threat posed by ISIL in Iraq and Syria. With a moto of *'One Mission, Many Nations', Operation Inherent Resolve* is an example of the way in which countries can work together in the pursuit of a common enemy. This is significant as it shows how coalition governmental actions can be employed to increase regional stability. This can have a positive impact on the international community as nations can all work together in their pursuit of a resolution to this complex international issue.

According to the U.S. State Department, there are currently 66 participants in the coalition, including Afghanistan, Albania, the Arab League, Australia, Austria, Bahrain, Belgium, Bosnia and Herzegovina, Bulgaria, Canada, Croatia, Cyprus, Czech Republic, Denmark, Egypt, Estonia, the European Union, Finland, France, Georgia, Germany, Greece, Hungary, Iceland, Iraq, Ireland, Italy, Japan, Jordan, Kosovo, Kuwait, Latvia, Lebanon, Lithuania, Luxembourg, Macedonia, Malaysia, Moldova, Montenegro, Morocco, The Netherlands, New Zealand, Nigeria, Norway, Oman, Panama, Poland, Portugal, Qatar, Republic of Korea, Romania, Saudi Arabia, Serbia, Singapore, Slovakia, Slovenia, Somalia, Spain, Sweden, Taiwan, Tunisia, Turkey, Ukraine, the United Arab Emirates, the United Kingdom and the United States.

Country contributions include both military and non-military assistance. Switzerland donated $9 million in aid to Iraq, Belgium contributed $15.5 million of humanitarian aid to Iraq, Italy contributed $2.5 million worth of weaponry (including machine guns, rocket-propelled grenades, and 1 million rounds of ammunition), while Japan's granted $6million in emergency aid to specifically help displaced people in Northern Iraq.

As part of CJTF-OIR, countries which have conducted airstrikes in Iraq include the United States, Australia, Canada, Belgium, Denmark, France, Jordan, the Netherlands, and the United Kingdom. Those who have conducted airstrikes in Syria include the United States,

Australia, Bahrain, Canada, Belgium, France, the Netherlands, Jordan, Saudi Arabia, Turkey, the United Arab Emirates, and the United Kingdom.

According to official reports, the Coalition conducted a total of 30,008 strikes between August 2014 and the end of August 2018. There have been some significant positive steps forward in tackling the threat of ISIL, notably the fact that more than 84,000 square kilometres once held by ISIL have been cleared of territory, more than 4 million people have been freed of ISIL control, almost 2 million people formerly displaced have returned to their homes in Iraq, and foreign fighters who once flowed into Iraq and Syria at hundreds per week have now slowed to a handful per month. This is significant as it shows that when countries work together, they can push back the creation of the Islamic caliphate and assist ordinary people caught in the cross-fire of ISIL's actions.

According to a 2016 report by the Congressional Research Service, the Coalition are also involved in the training, advising, assisting and equipment of Iraqi Security Forces. It has also trained more than 20,000 Peshmerga fighters of Iraq's Kurdistan Regional Government. This is significant as it shows that the Coalition has worked to try to create a long-term political solution to the scourge of terrorism by equipping local forces with the expertise required to safeguard the region in the future. This is important as it may allow these countries to be perceived as responsible and respectful of the futures of the countries affected. On the other hand, it could be argued that foreign intervention in an already volatile region could only fuel resentment towards the West and result in individuals becoming radicalised and joining terror groups as they seek revenge for military action and inevitable civilian casualties.

The Congressional Research Service Report of 2016 found that given that there is not a single authority responsible for prioritising military lines of effort, various state actors often work at cross-purposes without intending to do so. This is significant as it shows that there are coalition coordination challenges where some coalition partners have different, and often conflicting, longer-term regional geopolitical interests from those of the United States or other coalition members. This is significant as it may result in some partners advancing their own goals ahead of those of the coalition itself. This could result in a difficultly in consolidating gains and achieving campaign success.

2. RSII coalition, (Russia–Syria–Iran–Iraq coalition) also referred to as 4+1 (in which the "plus one" refers to Hezbollah of Lebanon)

Background to the international relations between these countries:

Russia has a long history and relationship with the Assad regime in Syria. Diplomatic relations between the Soviet Union and Syria were established in July 1944. In October

1980, Syria and the Soviet Union signed a Treaty of Friendship and Cooperation which provides for regular consultations on bilateral and multilateral issues of interest, coordination of responses in the event of a crisis, and military cooperation. Russian investments in Syria were valued at $19.4 billion in 2009, according to *The Moscow Times*, and according to a European Commission report its exports to Syria were worth $1.1 billion in 2010. Russia's only Mediterranean naval base for its Black Sea Fleet has been located in the Syrian port of Tartus since 1971. Syria also accommodates Russia's S400 air defence system in Latakia. According to *The New York Times*, from 2000 to 2010, Russia sold around $1.5 billion worth of arms to Syria. It is evident therefore that this strong bilateral relationship between the two countries is one based on economic, diplomatic and military mutual gain and goals.

Russia has launched airstrikes in Syria (against ISIL and the anti-Assad rebels fighting against Assad in the Syrian Civil War) from Iranian territory. Since the fall of the Soviet Union, Russia and Iran have enjoyed close relations. Iran and Russia are strategic allies. Due to Western economic sanctions on Iran, Russia has become an important trading partner, especially in relation to oil. Iran is the only country in Western Asia that has been invited to join the Collective Security Treaty Organization, Russia's own international treaty organization in response to NATO. The Iranian military are equipped with largely Russian weaponry. Following the 2015 Joint Comprehensive Plan of Action JCPOA agreement (also known as the Iran

Nuclear Deal), Russia agreed to the delivery of the S-300 missile defence system to Iran.

The New York Times reported in 2011 that Syria is Iran's "*closest ally*". The two countries have had a strategic alliance ever since the Iran–Iraq War (1980-88). Both countries have fractious relationships with both the United States and Israel. Israel and Syria have been in a state of war since the establishment of the State of Israel in May 1948. Syria and Israel have fought three major wars: the 1948 Arab Israeli War (1948), the Six-Day War (1967), and the Yom Kippur War (1973) They were both also involved in the Lebanese Civil War and the 1982 Lebanon War, as well as the War of Attrition (fighting between Israel and Egypt, Jordan, PLO and their allies from 1967 to 1970).

Syria cooperates with Iran by sending arms to Palestinian groups and Hezbollah in Lebanon. During the Syrian Civil War Iran, along with her 4+1 allies has been committed to keeping Assad in power. Iran, Syria, Iraq, and Russia also form an anti-terrorism alliance that has its headquarters in Baghdad. The United States and the United Kingdom have classified both Iran and Syria as 'State Sponsors of Terrorism'.

Hezbollah has long been an ally of the Ba'ath government of Syria. Hezbollah is a Shi'a Islamist political party and militant group based in Lebanon. Hezbollah has helped the Syrian government during the civil war in its fight against the Syrian opposition, which Hezbollah has described as a Zionist plot to destroy its alliance with Assad against Israel. One of the group's primary aims is the elimination of the State of Israel. This is motivated by the group's reaction to what it believes is Israel's illegal occupation of Lebanese territory. Lebanon considers the Shebaa Farms, a small strip of land on the Lebanese-Syrian border alongside the Israeli-occupied Golan Heights captured by Israel from Syria in the 1967 war, to be Lebanese territory. The international community do not recognise this territory as belonging to the State of Israel.

This shows that the 4+1 coalition is united by a hostile relationship towards the USA and Israel. It is also based on economic, military and diplomatic requirements.

The strategic priorities of the 4+1 coalition in Syria appear to fundamentally differ from those of the U.S.-led counter-ISIL coalition. It has been argued that the 4+1 coalition's actions in Syria are motivated not be a desire to eradicate ISIL, but instead by a desire to keep Assad in power and fight the rebels that oppose his rule. *Al Jazeera* reported in 2015 that 4+1 was formed as a consequence of an agreement reached at the end of September 2015 between Russia, Iran, Iraq and Syria to "*help and cooperate in collecting information about the terrorist Daesh group*" (ISIL) with a view to combatting the advances of the group. *Time* magazine reported in 2015 that the Syrian regime has purchased fuel from ISIL-controlled oil facilities and has maintained a relationship throughout the conflict. *Time* also reported that Assad is perhaps adopting a pragmatic approach towards ISIL as he does not consider the group to be his primary problem. Instead, Assad focuses his efforts and attention towards the Free Syrian Army and the

Al-Nusra Front as these groups are motivated solely by their goal of removing Assad from power.

It could be suggested that while coalitions may bring the international community together, the existence of CJTF-OIR and 4+1 only serve to create divisions and proxy wars as these countries fight each other and seem at odds in purpose. This will result in a disjointed political response and ultimately fractured international relations.

3. The Global Coalition

'The Global Coalition against Daesh' was formed in September 2014. theglobalcoalition.org reports that 79 coalition partners have committed themselves to the goals of eliminating the threat posed by ISIL and have already contributed in various capacities to the effort to combat ISIL in Iraq, the region and beyond. The Coalition works together to stabilise regions affected by ISIL, notably Iraq and Syria. It also works to dismantle the terror group's networks and counters its global ambitions of creating an Islamic caliphate. Work is ongoing to destroy ISIL's financing and economic infrastructure, preventing the flow of foreign terrorist fighters across borders, supporting stabilisation and the restoration of essential public services to areas liberated from ISIL and countering the group's propaganda.

$706m in humanitarian aid and stabilisation support was dispersed in Syria in 2017 by the Global Coalition.

Germany recently gave an additional €10m for demining in Raqqa. The UK also gave a £10m package to support the people of Raqqa. Led by the USA, over 830 metric tonnes of aid have been delivered to Raqqa alone.

124,000 Iraqi Security Forces have been trained by the Coalition while $581.4m in humanitarian aid and stabilisation was dispersed in Iraq in 2017. 1,144 stabilisation projects are currently ongoing in Iraq, coordinated by this coalition.

The Global Coalition's breadth and diversity of partners demonstrate the global and unified nature of this endeavour. Institutions such as the Arab League, Interpol, NATO and the European Union combine efforts with African nations such as Egypt and Libya, Asia Pacific countries such as Japan and Fiji, 25 European nations, and six Middle Eastern countries, the USA and Canada. This is significant as this combined counter-terrorism and stabilising effort will foster strong multi-lateral international relations. It could be argued that only by working together, the international community will be successful in pushing back the impact of ISIL in Iraq and Syria. The importance of regional and interregional cooperation in the fight against terrorism cannot be overstated. When these global partners work together the capacity to tackle and resolve terrorism will increase.

TACKLING TERRORISM

How effective is the UK Government in tackling the issue of terrorism?

FINANCIAL STRATEGIES

The UK Government has introduced a number of financial strategies designed to disrupt the finances of groups such as ISIL. The UK Government has public and private cooperation with the banking industry to ensure ISIL is denied access to the official financial system. This may be limited in its effectiveness because it has been reported that ISIL is funded in part by the Gulf States of Saudi Arabia and Qatar (although both states deny this accusation). Furthermore, Turkey and Syria have been accused of purchasing ISIL's oil. It has been estimated that ISIL generate up to $3 million USD per day in oil revenue although an accurate figure is almost impossible to provide given that much of their trading is on the black market and in cash. This means that even if the UK Government deny access to the official banking system for terror groups, they can receive funding elsewhere and so the impact of this strategy is severely limited.

The Al-Qaida (Asset Freezing) Regulations were introduced in 2011 by the UK Government. The UK Treasury has frozen bank accounts of individuals believed to be financing terror organisations. One such individual is Bilal Abdullah who rented a car used in the 7/7 London bombings and was the passenger in Glasgow airport attack in 2007. The freezing of assets is limited in its effectiveness as in 2011 only £72,000 had been frozen by the UK Treasury. This is not a significant amount of money when the scale and cost of funding international terrorism is considered. In addition, money can be moved through the informal Hawala finance network, commonly used by ISIL. This is a network of money brokers that is based on trust, reputation and honour. Through this system there is no actual physical transferal of cash and so this makes money impossible to track. The Asset Freezing regulations are therefore limited in their effectiveness as money moved in this way is untraceable.

The Money Laundering, Terrorist Financing and Transfer of Funds Regulations were introduced in 2017. The intention behind these regulations is to ensure that the financial system is too difficult an environment for illicit activities such as terrorism to develop and thrive. These regulations require data of the payer and payee. This could be an effective strategy for tackling terrorism as these strengthened rules improve transparency and make tracking and tracing money easier. However, if a terror supporter or financer wanted to send money via Western Union, they can make multiple £999 cash deposits without needing ID. In addition, some terrorist groups establish seemingly legitimate businesses, such as taxi firms and social clubs, through which cash can be laundered and then used for the purposes of both organised crime and international terrorism. The IRA used this strategy to raise funds for their acts of terrorism.

LEGISLATIVE STRATEGIES

In 2018 the Counter-Terrorism Border and Security Act was introduced by the UK Government. The purpose of this law was to amend certain terrorism offences for the digital age and to reflect contemporary patterns of radicalisation, increase the maximum penalty for certain offences, ensuring the punishment better reflects the crime and better prevents re-offending. It also makes provisions to manage offenders following their release from custody, strengthens the powers of the police to prevent and investigate terrorist offences and harden the UK's defences at the border against hostile state activity.

The maximum penalty for certain terrorism-related offences, such as the distribution of terrorist publications, will be increased to 15 years imprisonment. This could prove to be an effective strategy in the fight against terrorism as the increase in prison time may act as a deterrent. However, there is evidence to suggest that longer prison sentences are limited in their effectiveness as terrorists may not value their futures and many are prepared to die for their cause. If a terrorist does not expect to survive an attack the threat of a long prison sentence will not be a deterrent. Research by the GTI in 2018 reported that prisons provided a recruitment hub for terrorists. The GTI stated that there is *"the risk of terrorists acquiring followers who are experiencing periods of vulnerability and are susceptible to violent extremism. Prisoners can be radicalised by external means including books, videos, websites and visitors or by internal sources as well as fellow inmates"*. This could mean that the imprisonment of influential radical individuals under this new law may create a climate of radicalisation and even result in the creation of future terrorists. However, for those people who have become radicalised and are prepared to distribute terrorist material (but not carry out an attack), this new law may be effective as it could allow the security services to intercept and stop the spread of extremist material designed to incite terrorism and terror attacks. A potential issue with this strategy is that it could be perceived as limiting freedom of expression of inmates. Without adequate and sensitive training, some prison officers may interpret the possession of a religious book, such as the Qur'an, as extremist material. Many inmates turn to religion when incarcerated as a means to seek forgiveness for their crimes or as they may believe it provides them with a direction and moral framework. It could be the case that if some religious faiths are viewed with suspicion this may cause divisions and create a sense that one faith is under attack. This only serves to fuel the narrative of extremist groups who call to arms individuals to defend their faith.

The Counter Terrorism and Border Security Act (2018) also increases the time that the UK Government is able to retain fingerprints and DNA from 2 to 5 years in a case where a person has not been convicted of an offence. This may be effective in tackling terrorism as such biometrics can help to identify potential terrorists and allow security services to arrest quickly and with confidence persons of interest or concern. The human rights group, *Liberty*, argue that this is unethical and breaches the human rights of individuals not convicted of any crime as such a law may result in a breach of an individual's privacy. Some would argue that national security is being prioritised over human rights.

The Terrorism Act of 2000 has been recently amended to make it an offence to view or access terrorist material on line without an excuse. This may be effective in tackling terrorism as this law provides access to Internet search histories. These can be monitored and allow the security services (MI5 and GCHQ) to intercept someone at risk of radicalisation or someone who is inciting terrorism via social media. This could be effective as these powers could stop a potential terror attack or uncover the location of a terror cell through the tracking of IP (Internet Protocol) addresses as these reveal an individual's real-world location on the internet. It is possible, however, to disguise one's IP address using a Virtual Private Network (VPN) as this allows an individual to stay anonymous when online.

Other limitations of this amendment include the fact that terrorist recruiters can groom individuals on line in a very subtle manner and the individual may not even realise to whom they are chatting to in online forums or messaging on platforms such as Twitter. In addition, human rights groups have dubbed these powers 'Orwellian' as they perceive the UK Government to be trampling over individual rights, such as the right to freedom of speech.

MILITARY STRATEGIES

One form of military strategy is the direct attack of terrorists using drones or fighter aircrafts. In August 2018 there were two airstrikes recorded by the UK Government. Tornado fighter jets attacked a truck belonging to ISIL in northern Iraq and a building occupied by ISIL was demolished. In addition, a UK Reaper drone struck a terrorist-held building in Syria. As a result of such air strikes, the UK Government reports that ISIL has lost 90% of the territory that it controlled in 2014. This direct military action can be considered effective as the elimination of high value targets such as terrorist group leaders and other persons of concern can destabilise terror groups.

Such airstrikes have also been instrumental in the liberation of millions of people from the control of ISIL. Airstrikes can weaken terror groups numerically and destroy key strongholds. This can also serve to weaken the 'brand', grip on power and reach of the terror group which could then see a reduction in the number of new recruits. However, airstrikes can result in collateral damage – unintended civilian casualties caused by a military operation. The impact of this is that those who have lost loved ones in airstrikes may wish to seek vengeance causing a rise in terrorism rather than a reduction as intended.

The sharing of intelligence, surveillance and reconnaissance is a key military strategy employed by the UK Government. The Royal Airforce provides highly advanced intelligence to the UK's Global Coalition partners. Participating in the Global Coalition and the sharing of intelligence is an effective way to tackle terrorism as a collaborative and multilateral front allows for a unified response to terrorism. Intelligence sharing is an essential strategy for maintaining national and regional security. It could be argued that terrorism is rarely truly localised or confined to one nation but instead is linked to multiple countries and flows across borders.

CONTEST STRATEGY

The UK Government's counter-terrorism strategy is be organised around four workstreams, each comprising several key objectives:

- Pursue: to stop terrorist attacks;
- Prevent: to stop people becoming terrorists or supporting terrorism;
- Protect: to strengthen our protection against a terrorist attack;
- Prepare: to mitigate the impact of a terrorist attack.

According to the UK Government, the aim of CONTEST is to reduce the risk to the UK and its interests overseas from terrorism, so that people can go about their lives freely and with confidence.

The 'Prevent' strand of CONTEST tackles directly the possibility of radicalisation. The objectives of Prevent are *"to tackle the causes of radicalisation and respond to the ideological challenge of terrorism, safeguard and support those most at risk of radicalisation through early intervention, identifying them and offering support and enable those who have already engaged in terrorism to disengage and rehabilitate."* The Prevent programme is delivered with and through community groups and leaders, civil society organisations, public sector institutions including local authorities, schools and universities, health organisations, police, prisons and probation, and the private sector.

Since 1 July 2015 all schools, registered early years childcare providers and registered later years childcare providers are subject to a duty under section 26 of the Counter-Terrorism and Security Act 2015, in the exercise of their functions, to have *"due regard to the need to prevent people from being drawn into terrorism"*. This duty is known as the *Prevent duty*. The Prevent duty requires education providers to have clear policies in place to safeguard students and build their resilience to radicalisation in schools, further and higher education institutions. A network of Prevent Education Officers has been established which plays a key role in supporting schools in priority areas and informing the development of policy and practice nationally.

The Prevent strategy could be seen as an effective approach to tackle terrorism as it could potentially protect vulnerable individuals from being radicalised. The fact that key individuals, such as teachers, are tasked with monitoring the behaviours of young people, could be important given the amount of time that such professionals may spend with children. That said, it could be argued that the Prevent duty of teachers may serve to restrict debate and free speech in lessons. Young people are developing their beliefs and are faced with sensitive topics at a time in their lives in which they are trying to find their place in society and the world. It could be the case that some over-zealous teachers may misunderstand a pupil, and this could result in the pupil being reported and investigated without justifiable cause. Debates in lessons such as Modern Studies, Politics and PSE are fundamental in encouraging and challenging ideas and it would be a shame for pupils to fear speaking up or feel that they are being monitored. Schools should be a safe place in which pupils feel free to discuss a range of views and listen to those of their peers.

In addition, the Prevent duty states that teachers can safeguard vulnerable pupils against radicalisation by promoting *'fundamental British values'*. According to Ofsted, 'fundamental British values' are *"democracy, the rule of law, individual liberty, mutual respect for and tolerance of those with different faiths and beliefs and for those without faith"*. This has caused concern and controversy given that many teachers do not understand how to interpret this message of British values. It has been reported that some teachers believe it to mean stereotypical images of London buses and fish and chips whereas others have interpreted it to mean a celebration of Britain's imperial past. Such stereotypical images of Britain are damaging and do little to prevent radicalism. In fact, it could be argued that such an approach creates a 'them' and 'us' scenario where some pupils feel that they are viewed with suspicion by their teachers. Critics would argue that teachers' roles do not include the promotion of 'Britishness'. This can exclude those pupils and teachers not born in Britain and in the extreme any non-White individual. The fundamental values espoused by Ofsted are not exclusive to Britain. Values such as tolerance and respect are the values of other countries also. There is nothing particularly 'British' about these values – it defines and describes 'us' in comparison to 'them' who are not British. The significance of such an approach could be a polarisation of people, a lack of community cohesion, distrust and even a rise in radicalisation as some fear that their values are under attack or deemed not to be 'British'.

Considering that one of the most significant drivers of radicalisation and recruitment are political grievances, it seems that Prevent's focus on promoting British values will do very little to uncover radical elements in schools. Terrorist groups such as ISIL are motivated by vengeance for Western foreign policy that they believe has caused irreparable damage to the Middle East. They are also committed to creating a theocracy in the form of a caliphate based on Islamic values. It could be argued that the British values promoted by the UK Government only serve to enrage further such terror groups given the historic damage caused to the Middle East by Britain's imperial track record of intolerance, lack of respect for borders, tribes and Islamic values and individual liberty (The Sykes-Picot Agreement of 1916 being a clear example of this). Some terror groups would also argue that Britain's current action in Syria and Iraq (and the 2003 invasion of Iraq) are also examples of Britain imposing their 'values' on other nations. The implication of this is that those at risk of radicalisation may be motivated by British foreign policy actions and be driven by a desire to seek vengeance for perceived intolerance and aggression by Britain and other western powers. Promoting British values in schools though Prevent may have the reverse desired and intended effect and ultimately result in greater radicalisation.

How effective has the international community been in tackling the issue of terrorism?

The United Nations

The United Nations Office of Counter-Terrorism (UNOCT) was established in June 2017 and has five main functions:

1. *Provide leadership on the General Assembly counter-terrorism mandates entrusted to the Secretary-General from across the United Nations system;*
2. *Enhance coordination and coherence across the 38 Counter-Terrorism Implementation Task Force entities to ensure the balanced implementation of the four pillars of the UN Global Counter-Terrorism Strategy;*
3. *Strengthen the delivery of United Nations counter-terrorism capacity-building assistance to Member States;*
4. *Improve visibility, advocacy and resource mobilization for United Nations counter-terrorism efforts;*
5. *Ensure that due priority is given to counterterrorism across the United Nations system and that the important work on preventing violent extremism is firmly rooted in the Strategy.*

The United Nations Security Council Counter-Terrorism Committee (CTC) was established in the wake of the September 11, 2001 attacks in New York. The CTC is assisted by the Counter-Terrorism Committee Executive Directorate (CTED), which carries out the policy decisions of the Committee, conducts expert assessments of each

Member State and facilitates counter-terrorism technical assistance to countries.

In July 2018 the CTED alongside the United Nations Office on Drugs and Crime (UNODC) organised a regional workshop (funded by Japan) on developing approaches for the screening and prosecution of persons associated with Boko Haram. The countries of the region developed recommendations for coherent approaches in dealing with this challenge. These efforts are regarded as an essential step in equipping regional officials with the knowledge and tools needed to evaluate and process the large numbers of people currently detained, including how to determine who could be prosecuted for terrorism offences. This shows that the UN is working effectively to encourage collaboration by facilitating dialogue between UN member states. Through such workshops, the UN is able to direct and manage effective thinking about strategies and solutions to combat the threat and actions of terror groups, such as Boko Haram. Mr. Abdou Hamani, a senior judge from Niger and UNODC expert, noted that *"the adoption by participants of a template form to be used for screening by the Lake Chad Basin countries will help to significantly harmonize screening practices and facilitate the use of information contained therein in the criminal procedures."*

The UNOCT was invited by the Nigerian Government in July 2018 to assist in identifying concrete areas where the United Nations could provide technical assistance in order to enhance Nigeria's efforts to address the threat posed by

Boko Haram and other terrorist groups in the country and in the sub-region. The process took account of recommendations previously identified by the UN CTC and endorsed by the Government. High-ranking officials in Nigeria, including the Vice-President, Mr. Yemi Osinbajo, and key Ministers and heads of agencies, as well as the Chairman of the Human Rights Commission, civil society organisations, women's groups, the United Nations Country Team and representatives of the diplomatic community met to consider ways in which the National Counter Terrorism Strategy and Plan of Action could be rolled out in the region. By the end of the meeting there was a commitment by the UN to provide technical assistance in seven priority areas: the implementation of the National Action Plan in accordance with the UN Global Counter Terrorism Strategy; the prevention of violent extremism, and support to rehabilitation and reintegration processes; the provision of support to criminal justice processes, in compliance with the rule of law and human rights principles; the empowerment of women and girls to counter terrorism and violent extremism, aviation and maritime security, border management; and strategic communication to prevent violent extremism. This strategic support has been effective in pushing back the threat of Boko Haram and managing the prosecution of those associated with the group.

As a result of the Nigerian Government's efforts to tackle Boko Haram, in early 2018, U.S. President Donald J. Trump agreed a $600 million deal to sell 12 Super Tucano aircraft to Nigeria to support its counterterrorism efforts, thereby improving the bilateral diplomatic and trade relationship of the two countries. Boko Haram's influence has declined in recent years in part due to internal crises with the group itself which have enabled some insurgents to surrender, change side or engage in dialogue with the government. However, this decline could also be explained by the effective and active support of the UN which has allowed the Nigerian Government and its neighbours to try to resolve the threat and impact of Boko Haram. It could be argued that without this support, the group may have grown in influence and permeated multiple borders.

The European Union

The European Union Counter-Terrorism Strategy outlines the EU's strategic commitment to combat terrorism globally while respecting human rights. It also aims to make Europe safer by allowing EU citizens to live in area of freedom, security and justice.

The EU Strategy sets out four objectives to prevent new recruits to terrorism; *better protect potential targets; pursue and investigate members of existing networks and improve its capability to respond to and manage the consequences of terrorist attacks.* The EU works to strengthen national capabilities by using best practice and sharing knowledge and experiences to help EU countries respond to terrorism. It encourages the collection and sharing of intelligence to facilitate a coordinated counter-terrorism response. It works effectively by coordinating EU bodies including Europol, the EU's law enforcement agency headquartered in The Hague, the Netherlands. Europol assists the 28 EU

Member States in their fight against serious international crime and terrorism. The EU purports to believe strongly in collective European action and solidarity to combat terrorism.

The fight against terrorism in Europe has traditionally been the responsibility of individual EU member states, with security understood as a strictly national prerogative. But the European Union is now a genuine actor in the field of transnational threats management, according to online independent news source, *The Conversation.*

In early 2016, Europol introduced the European Counter Terrorism Center, which facilitates the exchange of intelligence and helps manage the European Bomb Data System (EBDS). In the event of an attack, its emergency response team (EMRT) becomes available to member states. This shows an effective response to tackling terrorism as these experts have been deployed to locations of European attacks, notably, the November 2015 Paris attacks.

The Paris attacks marked a watershed in terms of intelligence sharing within the EU. Europol reported in 2016 a 20% increase in the number of operational messages exchanged by 2014 and an increase of more than 60% in the Europol Information System (EIS) database. The number of persons known to have been foreign combatants and registered in Europol's database increased six-fold between 2015 and 2016.

The EU also works cooperatively to protect vulnerable targets such as transport networks, sporting events, shopping centres and schools. Those efforts resulted from a February workshop organised in the wake of the 2015 Thalys attack where a man opened fire on a Thalys train (French-Belgian High-Speed Train Operator) on its way from Amsterdam to Paris before his assault rifle jammed, and he was subdued by passengers, and the 2016 Brussels bombing. ISIL claimed responsibility for the Brussels bombing which included three coordinated suicide bombings; two at Brussels Airport, and one at Maalbeek metro station in central Brussels. 32 civilians and 3 perpetrators were killed, and more than 300 people were injured. The perpetrators had been part of the same terrorist cell that had conducted the November 2015 Paris attacks.

However, there have been reports that the EU's counter-terrorism response is limited in its effectiveness. A report on progress towards a "Security Union" reveals that EU measures have not been completely put in place by member states, reducing their effectiveness — for example, EU legislation intended to better control explosives. Even though the European Commission has made funds available to cover delays attributed to the costs of implementing EU legislation, the money available is not always fully used by them.

The "Prüm project", was intended to facilitate the exchange of vehicle registration, fingerprint and DNA data among EU members. The Prüm framework outlines provisions under which EU Member States grant each other access to their automated DNA analysis files, automated fingerprint identification systems and vehicle registration data. DNA and fingerprint exchanges take place based on a "hit/no-hit" approach, which means that DNA profiles or fingerprints found at a crime scene in one EU Member State can be compared automatically with profiles held in the databases of other EU States. Car registration data (including licence plates and chassis numbers) are exchanged through national platforms that are linked to the online application "EUCARIS". The "Prüm project" was supposed to have been implemented by all member states in August 2011. However, by the spring of 2015 several Member States had not yet fulfilled their legal obligations under the Prüm Decision. This shows that the EU may not be entirely effective in tackling terrorism as the counter-terrorism strategy is only viable if all member states cooperate and work collaboratively.

The decision on whether the UK would seek to join the Prüm exchange was debated in Parliament on 8th December 2015 (The UK exercised its right to opt-out of the exchange from 2014). Following research with stakeholders and partners within the UK Criminal Justice System and across the EU a Home Office led pilot (which exchanged over 2,500 DNA profiles with selected EU member states) Parliament voted in favour of the Government's motion to join the Prüm exchange. This shows that when member states work together, they can build the capacity to tackle terrorism. Sharing intelligence will speed up the detection of those suspected of planning or those who have committed acts of terror. This will enable security services to intercept individuals before they are able to conduct acts of terror or prevent them from committing further atrocities, thereby safeguarding lives.

The European Arrest Warrant (EAW), introduced in January 2004, allows for a court within an EU state to issue a request to get a suspect extradited. The EAW means mutual recognition of criminal justice systems in the EU. This can be a very effective strategy to tackle international terrorism as it fosters strong cross-border counter-terrorism policing. This means that suspects accused of terrorism related offences (or accused of any offence incurring a maximum penalty of at least a year in prison or must have been already sentenced to at least four months in prison) can be intercepted and brought to justice in the country that has been directly impacted by a terror plot or act. Whether the UK will still benefit from the EAW following its departure from the EU, remains unclear at the time of publication.

North Atlantic Treaty Organisation

At the July 2016 Summit of Heads of State and Government in Warsaw, NATO reaffirmed its commitment to fighting terrorism and supporting the counter-IS coalition (Global Coalition). NATO's work on counter-terrorism focuses on improving awareness of the threat, developing capabilities to prepare and respond, and enhancing engagement with partner countries and other international actors.

The alliance agreed that its Airborne Warning and Control System (AWACS) would provide valuable support to coalition members. NATO operates a fleet of Boeing E-3A AWACS aircraft, with their distinctive radar domes mounted on the fuselage, which provide the Alliance with air surveillance, command and control, battle space management and communications. This is an effective response to tackling the threat of terrorism because it provides surveillance and situational awareness to the Global Coalition to Defeat ISIS, thereby making the skies safer.

NATO has also expanded its current training mission for Iraqi officers, which is currently based in Jordan, into Iraq itself. This has proven to be an effective response as it has allowed NATO to contribute to the stabilisation of the region after three years of war against ISIL.

NATO's Defence Against Terrorism Programme of Work (DAT POW) was set up to prevent non-conventional attacks, such as suicide attacks with improvised explosive devices (IEDs), and mitigate other challenges, such as attacks on critical infrastructure. Successful DAT POW projects include technologies to defend against mortar attacks, precision air drop technologies and protection of harbours and ports. This is an effective and important response as global trade is heavily dependent on shipping. This means that ports and harbours are attractive targets for terrorists as they can enact devastating and economically disruptive attacks from high-explosives to radiological bombs, even nuclear devices. In 1998 Al-

Qaeda used a cargo vessel to transport explosives for its attacks on US embassies in Kenya and Tanzania. Only about 5% of containers arriving in US ports are routinely screened with X-ray and gamma-ray devices therefore NATO's work is essential in the fight against terrorism.

Cyber defence is part of NATO's core task of collective defence. NATO Cyber Rapid Reaction teams are on standby to assist Allies, 24 hours a day, if requested and approved. NATO has been responsible for creating the Malware Information Sharing Platform (MISP), the Smart Defence Multinational Cyber Defence Capability Development (MN CD2) project, and the Multinational Cyber Defence Education and Training (MN CD E&T) project. This is significant because the cyber defence work of NATO enables member countries to work together to develop and maintain capabilities, they may not be able to afford to develop or procure independently, and to free resources for developing other capabilities. NATO is also effective in helping member countries by sharing information and best practices, and by conducting cyber defence exercises to help develop national expertise. This all contributes to a clearer strategic response to tackling international cyber terrorism

The proliferation of weapons of mass destruction (WMD) and their delivery systems are also a focus of NATO. The threat of bio-terrorism is one that is taken very seriously by NATO. The mission of NATO's Combined Joint Chemical, Biological, Radiological and Nuclear Defence Task Force (CBRN) is to provide a rapidly deployable defence capability against bio-terrorism. Chemical, biological, radiological and nuclear (CBRN) weapons are among the most dangerous weapons in the world. Several terrorist groups have actively sought weapons of mass destruction as they can cause a higher mortality than conventional weapons. NATO actively train first responders to tackle such an attack. It has been reported that terror groups such as ISIL has used both mustard gas and chlorine gas against Kurdish Peshmerga fighters in Iraq. ISIL has also conducted research into the development of radiological dispersion devices. The fear is that they may combine their CBR weapons knowledge with the use of small drones to devastating effect. Therefore, the work and activities of NATO's CBRN Task Force is essential as the expertise of terrorists grows and develop.

Operation Sea Guardian, launched in November 2016 carries out maritime security capacity building, and provides support to maritime situational awareness and to maritime counter-terrorism. Activities involve the planning and conduct of a range of operations to deter, disrupt, defend and protect against maritime-based terrorist activities. This operation could be highlighted as an effective response to tackling international terrorism as these monitoring activities aim to deny terrorists access to designated areas and contain threats through the use of force.

In July 2018 US President, Donald Trump, stated that many NATO members were not contributing funds that they had pledged. In 2002 a guideline (non-binding) was put forward to NATO members to contribute 2% of their GDP to collectively share the burden of defence costs. The U.S. accounts for 22% of the NATO alliance's common funding, which is spent on projects like military readiness, joint exercises, and initiatives to counter cyber-warfare. Trump came close to suggesting that the USA may withdraw from NATO if other member states failed to dramatically increase their financial contributions to the organisation. Although Trump cannot withdraw the USA from NATO with an executive order, bypassing US Congress, he has caused consternation among NATO members that withdrawal could even be a possibility.

The Guardian reported that the US leaving NATO would be a "*seismic step, previously unthinkable, that would shake up a western alliance that has endured for more than 70 years.*" If Trump does follow through with the threat to withdraw US NATO funding, the organisation will struggle to maintain operations such *as Operation Sea Guardian* and this will mean that NATO will become obsolete and this may leave the air, land and sea vulnerable to terrorism.

Acknowledgements

Institute for Economics & Peace. Global Terrorism Report 2018: Measuring and understanding the impact of terrorism, Sydney, November 2018.

Available from: http://visionofhumanity.org/reports (accessed December 2018)

About the author

Hannah Young has worked as a secondary school teacher for 15 years teaching History, Politics, Modern Studies and Philosophy.

Other titles by this author:

Higher Modern Studies: Social Inequalities in the UK Course Notes (June 2017) ISBN-10: 1792923384

46075559R00054

Printed in Poland
by Amazon Fulfillment
Poland Sp. z o.o., Wrocław